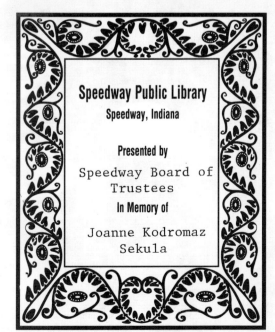

Planet Vegas

This book was made possible by the generous assistance of the following organizations:

CONVENTION AND VISITORS AUTHORITY

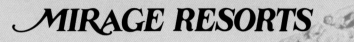

Additional sponsorship was generously provided by:

THE HOWARD HUGHES CORPORATION℠

NEVADA POWER COMPANY

RenoAir
Winning The West Over

Ethel·M
chocolates

PAULSON
GAMING SUPPLIES

Rio
SUITE HOTEL & CASINO
LAS VEGAS

Kodak

First Interstate Bank

Value
Rent·A·Car

Sunrise
HOSPITAL & MEDICAL CENTER

SUNDANCE
HELICOPTERS

Pages 4–5: Sidewalk palms, white canopies,
Tivoli lights, black stretch limos—Rodeo Drive in
Beverly Hills, right? Look again. The Golden
Nugget Hotel, situated in the heart of Glitter
Gulch, has all that *and* the world's largest gold
nugget, weighing in at 61 pounds.

Rick Browne

Pages 6–7: Fire and water. The fountain in front
of The Mirage erupts into flames every 15
minutes. The building of The Mirage catalyzed
the latest Las Vegas boom. When this
megaresort opened in November 1989, it was the
first new hotel to be built on the Strip in 16 years,
and triggered a building frenzy that stands at nine
megaresorts (and counting), the tallest observation tower in the country, a remake of downtown, a dozen neighborhood casinos, and
countless expansions and remodelings.

Paul Chesley

Pages 8–9: "Rockettes in Red," the opening number
of the Great Radio City Music Hall Spectacular,
performed in the Flamingo Hilton showroom.

Andy Levin

This page: A seldom seen view across the glass
pyramid of the Luxor.

Galen Rowell

Pages 12–13: The "video wall" in the MGM
Grand lobby consists of 80 screens driven by four
computers, 18 laser disk players, and just a
fraction of the 12 million feet of wire required to
turn on the largest hotel in the world.

Michael Yamashita

Pages 14–15: McCarran International now handles
half a million flights a year, making it the eighth
busiest airport in the world. From the runways
and the terminals, most eyes are drawn directly to
the pyramid-shaped Luxor hotel.

Alex Webb

First published in 1995 by Collins Publishers San Francisco,
1160 Battery Street, San Francisco, CA 94111

Planet Vegas / by 20 of the world's leading photographers ; [edited by] Rick
Browne and James Marshall.
              p.   cm.
      ISBN 0-00-225120-5
      1. Las Vegas (Nev.)—Pictorial works. I. Browne, Rick.   II. Marshall,
James, 1955- .
F849.L35P58 1995
979.3' 135—dc20   95-21913

Design: Tom Morgan, Blue Design, San Francisco, California
Printed in China

10 9 8 7 6 5 4 3 2

Planet Vegas

DIRECTED AND EDITED BY
RICK BROWNE & JAMES MARSHALL

INTRODUCTION BY
KENNY ROGERS

A PORTRAIT OF LAS VEGAS BY 20 OF THE WORLD'S LEADING PHOTOGRAPHERS

CollinsPublishersSanFrancisco
A Division of HarperCollinsPublishers

Planet Vegas Photographers

Susan Biddle	Robert Maass
Rick Browne	James Marshall
Paul Chesley	Claus Meyer
Michael Coyne	Galen Rowell
Neil Farrin	Jeffery Allan Salter
Jeff Gale	Alex Webb
Acey Harper	Nik Wheeler
Robert Holmes	Nevada Wier
Andy Levin	Michael Yamashita

Nik Wheeler

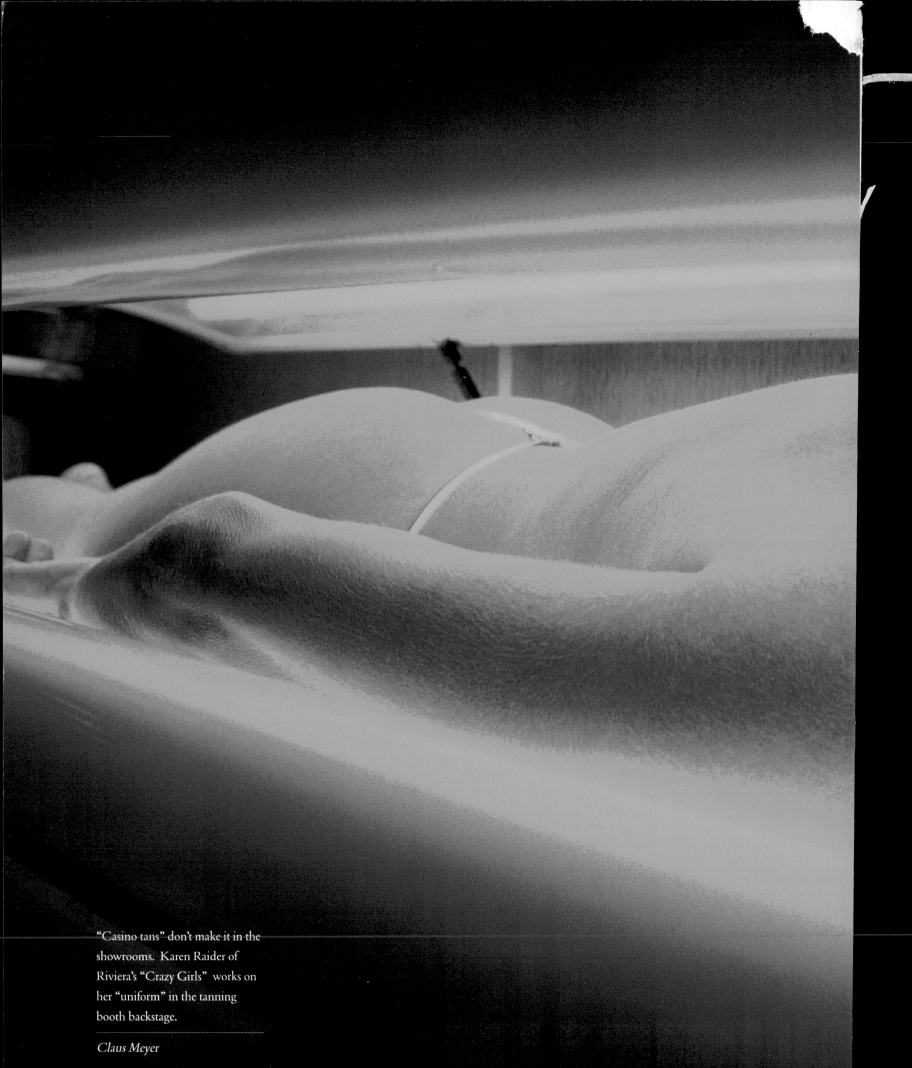

"Casino tans" don't make it in the
showrooms. Karen Raider of
Riviera's "Crazy Girls" works on
her "uniform" in the tanning
booth backstage.

Claus Meyer

THE MIRAGE

SIEGFRIED & ROY

Come see the
Royal White Tigers of
Siegfried & Roy.

Free admission 24 hours a day.

Perhaps the most legendary stretch
of road in the world, the Las
Vegas Strip is home to eleven of
the fourteen largest hotels in the
world: MGM Grand (1st),
Excalibur (3rd), Flamingo Hilton
(4th), The Mirage (6th), Treasure
Island (7th), Bally's (8th), Circus
Circus (9th), Imperial Palace
(10th), Luxor (12th), Stardust
(13th), and Riviera (14th).

Michael Coyne

Welcome to Planet Vegas

Kenny Rogers

As far back as I can recall, I've had a passion for Las Vegas. When I was younger, Las Vegas embodied a full-strength, hot-blooded, Wild West dream of mine, so it's no accident that my connection to the place spans more than three decades, practically my entire career. I first appeared on a Las Vegas stage in 1960 with the Bobby Doyle III and again a few years later with my own group, the First Edition. I was even entertainment director at the Golden Nugget Hotel for a while. And now I make my home here.

No other city I know feels so alive, so charged up with energy. You can hear the excitement, smell the money, taste the adventure, cut the action with a knife. Music bursts through the walls of every showroom, lounge, and bar. Some people find it too intense, but it brings out the West in me.

There's still a frontier presence in this city, a sense that Las Vegas'

Wild West past will always be an essential part of its present and future. I feel it when I go downtown where it all began or when I pass through the older casinos, some of which still have the original landscaping and low-rise motel rooms. I feel it when I see a sign that has survived the bygone days, telling its own story.

Old-timers, who hang on to the "good old days" like a familiar tune that rattles around in the memory, speak of dustier times when Las Vegas was a railroad town. I've heard tales about traveling salesmen, itching to try their luck, who jumped off the steam train while it was taking on water and ran into town for a shot of whiskey and a game of faro. The names of the drinks and games are certainly more sophisticated today, but people back then had the same idea about playing the edge.

In 1931, a bunch of gutsy legislators legalized wide-open gambling to help Nevada get through the Great Depression, but I doubt those lawmakers could have imagined the likes of Bugsy Siegel and his pals running the show for twenty years until Howard Hughes showed up. Hughes bought a bunch of casinos with legitimate money and cleaned up the town, but not a lot of people know that. He stayed around for just a few years, and after he left only one casino was built in Las Vegas for another two decades. Then Steve Wynn came along and built The Mirage and started a boom. That was in 1989, and Las Vegas is still booming and changing so fast that it's anyone's guess where imagination and technology are going to take it.

I spend a lot of time on the road on business or performing, but when I get home to Las Vegas, I hardly recognize the place! It's practically exploding at the seams, with fifty thousand or so people moving here every year. Las Vegas' population just hit a million. It has ninety thousand hotel rooms and gets nearly thirty million visi-

Frank Sinatra

By Kenny Rogers

Sammy Davis, Jr.

By Kenny Rogers

times it's hard to tell what's a deal and what's not. Or, for that matter, what's real and what's not.

Let's face it. There's no place anywhere quite like Las Vegas. Even with the growing popularity of gaming around the country, this city remains one of a kind. While other gambling destinations try to copy Vegas, they simply don't have the history or the mystery to pull it off. That's one of the things you'll discover as you explore this fascinating collection of photographs.

Photography is a passion that I've pursued for over twenty years. I've always felt that there are three ways to photograph people; the way they see themselves, the way others see them, and the way they've never been seen before. The same could well be said about photographing a place as diverse as Las Vegas.

It gives me great pleasure to be a part of a project in which twenty top photographers from around the world photographed this city from every angle imaginable, recording the dazzle as well as the everyday, the neon and the porch lights, the poker players and the softball players—in essence capturing on film the very heartbeat of this spectacular and complex city.

Like the title implies, this book brings down to earth a place that's out of this world.

tors each year—more than 80,000 people every day. That's like every man, woman, and child from Scranton, Pennsylvania, picking up and visiting Las Vegas every day of the week.

And no wonder. This place has everything. The largest hotel in the world. The tallest observation tower in the country. World-class entertainment that you can see for half the price you'd pay anywhere else. The most inexpensive restaurant food in the world. Scenic surroundings from Valley of Fire to Red Rock Canyon. A dozen or so spectacular golf courses. Shopping, people watching, roller coasters, you name it. Not to mention tens of thousands of slot machines and thousands of gaming tables. And the brightest spotlight in the world calling attention to it all.

Variety. That's a big part of what Las Vegas offers. Of course, there's plenty of irony in this city, too. We've all heard the one about the guy who went to a casino coffee shop for 99¢ bacon-and-eggs and fed $20 into a video poker machine on the way out. Some-

Welcome to Planet Vegas.

Kenny Rogers

Polishing the brass columns at
The World of Caesars Pavilion, the
first theme attraction in Las Vegas.
The Pavilion revolutionized local
design ideas and began a trend that
features theme park technology
aimed at adults. The elegant
portal, designed by Landmark
Entertainment, is one of the most
photographed sites in the city,
drawing as many as 12,000 people a
day through its Roman gateway
into Caesars Palace.

Michael Coyne

Top Caesars Palace brass welcomes visitors as they pass underneath flames and charging steeds to enter the ancient Roman-style casino.

Claus Meyer

Trying to cram all of Las Vegas into the average four-day stay can turn a trip into a frenzied whirlwind of neon sensations.

George Olson

"**L**ammers" denote the $20 and $100 denominations of "wheel chips" that roulette dealers use to distinguish among various players' bets.

Nevada Wier

Players and dealers are all over the layout in this view of a crap table via a one-way ceiling mirror.

Nik Wheeler

The ceiling bubble reflecting these roulette tables houses a lens connected by fiber optics to video monitors and recorders in the casino surveillance room. Every inch of the casino is under surveillance by these "eyes in the sky."

Nevada Wier

Slots are usually a solitary experience – until you line up a trio of sevens, then everyone wants to share the excitement. Here locals Lynda Smith and Kevin Steele jump for joy when they hit the triple digits, their one quarter bet paying an 80-quarter jackpot (or $20).

Rick Browne

For the first time ever, a woman, Barbara Enright, makes it to the final table at the World Series of Poker, the most prestigious gaming tournament in the world. The 1995 champion, Dan Harrington (center/left with glasses), is on his way to the million-dollar first prize.

James Marshall

ABOVE

A slot player reflects on what might have been (the previous pull) and ponders what might be (the next pull). Slot players now make up almost 65% of all casino gamblers.

Nevada Wier

RIGHT

"**S**itting box" at the Four Queens. The boxman oversees the action and is the highest authority on a dice table, settling disputes about rules, payoffs, and mistakes.

Nik Wheeler

The 4,000-square-foot
stained-glass dome above the pit
at the Tropicana is so delicate that
it's suspended on pneumatic
shock absorbers to safeguard it
from the vibrations of the
building's air conditioners. The
dome remains stationary and the
casino throbs around it.

Robert Holmes

Video poker may be the most
perfect gambling game ever
devised. It's fast (like craps).
There's control (like blackjack).
It's unintimidating and has a big
jackpot (like slots). And the risk
can be small (quarters, nickels,
even pennies).

Nevada Wier

Waiting for a tour bus to Hoover Dam. Local sights such as the dam, Lake Mead, and Red Rock lure visitors from around the world into the sunlight and Mother Nature's bounty just outside the city limits.

Susan Biddle

In Las Vegas, slot and video poker machines can be found at mini-marts, laundromats, supermarkets, drugstores, pizza parlors, restaurants and bars, even the airport.

Michael Coyne

Desert storm. Although the average annual rainfall is a mere four inches, a heavy storm can snarl traffic all over town, especially on the Strip. Slippery roads, poor drainage, and flash floods can wreak havoc during rush hour. But then, an hour or two later, the sun breaks through, clouds burn off, and it's as if nothing was ever wet. The sign at left advertises the incredible collection of priceless historic cars at the Imperial Palace hotel.

Jeffery Salter

John and Edna Luckman started the Gamblers Book Club in 1964; it's now the world's largest bookstore devoted to gambling. Pictured here is research director Howard Schwartz, born in Brooklyn, former reading teacher and sports writer, and renowned in the industry as the "gamblers' librarian."

Robert Maass

Johnny Tocco, owner of the famous Las Vegas boxing gym where champions train. The no-frills, hammer-it-out, closed-to-the-public sparring gym is the choice of many champions, who prefer to train in private.

Andy Levin

Crazy girls! On weekends, Stacey Petteruti is a principal dancer in the Riviera's "Crazy Girls," possibly the most risqué show on the Strip. During the week she teaches at her own studio, the Lakes School of Dance.

Claus Meyer

Kindergartners happily (well, most of them) rehearse for their graduation ceremony at Fong Elementary School. Clark County's school district is among the ten largest in the country. It encompasses nearly 8,000 square miles (larger than New Jersey) and serves more than 160,000 students. The district built 57 new schools between 1990 and 1994.

Jeffery Salter

LEFT

A poignant moment at the afternoon ballet class at Fern Adair's Conservatory of the Arts.

Nevada Wier

ABOVE

Children rehearse for a performance at Sign Design Theater, a group that combines American Sign Language with the performing arts to educate the hearing public about deaf culture and promote the self-esteem of hearing impaired group members.

Susan Biddle

Game playing comes naturally to these young Las Vegans. The Fong Elementary Dragon Chess Team won the 1995 Nevada Team Title in the 7th grade-and-under competition.

Jeffery Salter

This pickup truck was converted from gasoline to electric power by students from the Academy of Mathematics, Science, and Applied Technology magnet program at Clark High School. Nevada Power provided the truck and technical expertise, and students monitor the performance of the vehicle, now a part of Nevada Power's fleet.

Acey Harper

Emu farmer by day, Las Vegas
Thunder goalie by night, Clint
Malarchuk survived an accidental
severing of his jugular by an
opponent's skate blade and went
on to help the Thunder achieve
the best record in the International Hockey League in its
inaugural season.

Claus Meyer

Cool job! Lifeguards Melanie Darden and Mary Youshock, both 17, refresh themselves under a wall of water at Wet 'n Wild, the water park on the Strip.

Jeffery Salter

Chimney sweep Robert Koehne in traditional uniform prepares to swab a flue in the midst of Las Vegas' sprawling eastern suburbs.

Michael Coyne

P R E V I O U S
P A G E S

Expensive houses grace the shores of manmade lakes in the master-planned community of Desert Shores. In the distance is Summerlin, a 22,000-acre development on the west side of Las Vegas Valley. The land was purchased by Howard Hughes in the 1950s and is now one of the country's largest single ownership properties near a major metropolitan area. When the Hughes Corporation completes the build-out by the year 2015, 180,000 residents will occupy 30 distinct neighborhoods.

James Marshall

A B O V E

Las Vegas's population explosion has created jobs, especially for construction workers and others in the home-building industry.

Robert Maass

R I G H T

The city's perimeter line changes daily as new housing springs up to accommodate an influx of 4,000-6,000 new residents every month. When completed, this development will provide housing for but three days' worth of families moving to Las Vegas.

Rick Browne

Wanna play The Mirage's ultra-exclusive Shadow Creek Golf Course? Just get a million-dollar casino credit line. Only five or six highroller foursomes are scheduled on the course every day.

Michael Yamashita

A lone Joshua tree stands sentinel over the 18-hole, par-72 Nu-Wav Kaiv Golf Course at the Las Vegas Paiute Resort on reservation land north of the city.

Claus Meyer

Switzerland? Boulder, Colorado? No, it's the western suburbs of Las Vegas butting up against the Spring Mountains. The snowy peak is Mt. Charleston, fourth tallest mountain in Nevada. At the 9,000-foot level is Ski Lee, a downhill skiing resort less than an hour from the neon desert city.

Paul Chesley

Hoover Dam is one of the manmade wonders of the world. It's 726 feet high, 660 feet thick at its base (wider than two football fields), and holds back an estimated 50 trillion pounds of water in Lake Mead, one of the largest reservoirs in the world. Though the dam's 17 giant turbines generate enough electricity for half a million homes it only supplies four percent of Las Vegas' power needs, as Las Vegas is allocated only 12% of the dam's total capacity.

Claus Meyer

This map of the power grid is at Nevada Power's central dispatch center, where every hour of every day employees monitor system components to coordinate the changing customer demand for electricity.

Michael Coyne

Eleven thousand miles of power lines deliver 12 million megawatt hours of electricity to Nevada Power Company's 428,000 customers in the desert City of Lights and vicinity.

Claus Meyer

Doug Erosky from Sign Systems Inc. maintains the pink neon plumage adorning the facade of the Flamingo Hilton, the fourth largest hotel in the world.

James Marshall

The rainbow mushroom facade of the Westward Ho, the world's largest motel, creates a colorful court in the evening on Las Vegas' famed "Strip."

Alex Webb

YESCO's (Young Electric Sign Company) "boneyard" is the resting place of old signs which once lit up the Las Vegas night. Today they're antiques—used in advertising and fashion shoots, as background in commercials and rock videos, and as a curiosity to those interested in the history of Las Vegas signage.

Nik Wheeler

"The King" was the king of Las Vegas throughout the early '70s. Elvis debuted at the New Frontier in 1956, but didn't return until 1969, when he played the International (purchased soon after by Hilton). The triumphant comeback led to Elvis' nearly decade-long stint as the Las Vegas Hilton's premier headliner, and he performed in 144 sold-out shows. Las Vegas is the mecca of Elvis impersonators. Johnny Nenhagen (left) and George Helm (right), in costume, at a gathering of disciples.

Andy Levin

(Below) Selwyn Harris does his best high-flying Elvis/James Brown impersonation after leaping from the platform of A.J. Bungee.

Nevada Wier

A papier mâché Elvis and Hobbes front the entrance to the library at the Las Vegas Academy of International Studies, Performing and Visual Arts, a magnet school in the old Las Vegas High School building.

Nik Wheeler

(Above) Trent Carlini has hit the jackpot of Elvis impersonation: he's the final act in "Legends in Concert" at Imperial Palace.

Neil Farrin

(Left) Joe Baker impersonates Elvis impersonators, parodying the parody, in "Viva Las Vegas" at the Sands.

Robert Maass

(Next Page) Jesse Garin cruises the Strip in his pink cadillac

Andy Levin

Las Vegas's diverse entertain-ment mix includes male strip shows such as "Manpower Australia—The Thunder from Down Under," which performs to packed mainly female audiences at the Stardust.

Michael Coyne

Las Vegas showgirls have long epitomized elegance and glamour.

Jeff Gale

In a city known for its voracious appetite for showgirl wigs, even tinfoil creations sometimes do the trick.

James Marshall

Showgirl portrait; 25 of Las Vegas' most glamorous showgirls from 13 major production shows pose on the "Legends In Concert" stage at Imperial Palace. The ladies and their affiliations: Brandi Rochelle and Coty Alexander, "American Super‑stars," Luxor; Nicole Ginnie and Paige Woodward, "Legends in Concert," Imperial Palace; Marianne Slama, "Hot Rock N Country," The Plaza; Gracie Lund and Aleksandra Marinic, "La Cage," Riviera; Kelly Steinfort and Lara Chamberlin, "Enter The Night," Stardust; Cynthia Brimball and Delia Sheppard, "Splash II," Riviera; Christine Perchetti and Anneli Walmsley, "Folies Bergere," Tropicana; Anna Cooke and Sara Jurco, "Copacabana," Rio Suites; Cindy Padgett and Jennifer Turner, "Naughty Ladies Revue," Arizona Charlie's; Karen Raider and Stacey Petteruti, "Crazy Girls," Riviera; Amber Lea Hafen and Laranne Millonzi, "Country Tonite," Aladdin; Andrea Goettsche and Kristen Vierthaler, "Glitz," Sands; Gina Capecci and Toni Lee, "Rock Around the Clock," MGM Grand.

Rick Browne

Performing nightly in the main showroom of her own casino, Debbie Reynolds personally maintains the Las Vegas star-policy tradition that's slowly giving way to production shows and extravaganzas.

Susan Biddle

After the show, the unsinkable Debbie meets customers for pictures, auto-graphs, and chitchat. Her hands-on management style and a $30 million collection of movie memorabilia have helped the casino become popular with many fans.

Susan Biddle

"**A**merican Superstars" at Luxor is a high-octane star-impersonator show. "Little Richard" (left) belts out a tune while tinkling the ivories as he gets the crowd revved up for the fiddle-smoking Charlie Daniels (above) impersonator, Johnny Potash. Potash is the reigning Nevada fiddle-playing champion.

Rick Browne

It's rare to see child performers on the Las Vegas strip, but 10-year-old Katie Kern sings and dances in "Country Tonite" at the Aladdin. Katie is pictured here before the show getting ready in the dressing room, during the show performing with champion clogger (and show choreographer) Jon Burdette, and catching up on homework. A native Las Vegan, multi-talented Katie is also a yodeler and ventriloquist, clothes designer and seamstress, and straight A student.

Robert Holmes

In Las Vegas, you can get married by a Deputy Justice of the Peace or an Elvis impersonator, in a chapel or while bungee jumping, in your car, on a roller coaster, or in a hot-air balloon above the Strip, complete with a minister, video cameraman, and organist.

Robert Holmes

A B O V E

License plate on the van that transports couples to and from the Little White Chapel in the Sky

Robert Holmes

R I G H T

Filling out the paperwork, for a drive-up wedding, to say the least, of a casual sort.

Michael Coyne

"**W**e are gathered here today at the drive-up wedding window..." When the Nevada Legislature approved a scandalously short six-week residency requirement for granting divorces in 1931, it also authorized easy marriages: no blood test and no waiting period.

Michael Yamashita

Newlyweds Greg and Birgit Marshall sip Crystal champagne in a white convertible limousine in front of a castle on their fairy-tale wedding day.

Michael Yamashita

ABOVE

Today, the wedding industry is big business in Las Vegas, where approximately 85,000 couples tie the knot every year. To handle the crowds, the county Marriage License Bureau is open 24 hours on weekends and holidays to accommodate people from all over the world who want to get "hitched in Vegas."

Andy Levin

RIGHT

A "kiss for luck" between newlyweds after their Treasure Island Hotel chapel wedding.

Acey Harper

Casinos offer a game for every frame of mind. The "wheel of fortune" is a social game, where players raise a ruckus as the big wheel spins out another winner.

Robert Maass

R I G H T

Roulette players have a limited amount of time to place their wagers on the layout. Here they make a mad dash with their chips as the little white ball gets ready to settle on the winning number.

Robert Maass

R I G H T

A gaming table dealer serves up a winning smile.

Robert Maass

RACE 1 OFFICIAL
SWEET DOVE
H GARCIA   13.20 5.60 2.60
AFTER FOUR
R FIGUEROA   5.80 2.60
DANCETOTHELINE
R MARS   2.20

82 EXA 2/3   42.40
82 TRK 0   22.40

RACE 2 OFFICIAL
NEW FORBES
J BADILLA   15.60 6.60 3.80
ROBERT
R PFAU   6.60 3.20
MAJORED NATURAL
D GLADNEY   8.60

82 EXA 10/6   23.20
82 MIL 2/1   54.60
82 DBL 2/18   40.20
82 TRK 0   15.40

RACE 3 OFFICIAL
AUDREY JEAN
P SANCHEZ   15.60 6.60 3.80
PLEASURE REQUEST
R MARS   3.60 2.40
AILENA AIA
J FUENTES   3.00

82 EXA 2/5   23.40
82 EXA 5/2   54.60
82 TRK 0   169.60

RACE 4 OFFICIAL
MISS JR
D STIMPSON   6.20 3.80 2.40
SECRET TERIS
R DIDERICK   4.60 3.40
BOSON BUDDIES
J YORKUN   4.60

82 EXA 4/2   20.00
82 PK3 18/6/4   173.00
82 TRK 0   15.60

RACE 5 OFFICIAL
LIL CONTESSA
R PFAU   28.00 12.40 6.80
WINDS EXCHANGE
J SCOTT   6.00 3.60
FILLING LATE
P SANCHEZ   10.60

82 DBL 1/6   50.60
82 EXA 6/1   173.00
82 TRI 6/1/8   681.00

RACE 6 POST 0119
BOBS PIZZA PIE
K DIDERICK 124
ADDED ALIBI
J BADILLA   124
WHEEL EM AGAIN
R SEVILLE   124
POLAR ORBIT
J CREAGER   124
EL PRISIONERO
J YORKUN   124
MR ROMANTICO
E GARCIA   124

WELCOME TO THE MIRA

LATE SCR Moss   LATE SCR Moss   LATE SCR Moss   LATE SCR Moss   950 YDS GTR
                                                                          3YO (CLM)
Moss   LATE SCR Moss   LATE SCR 7   LATE SCR Moss

LOS ALAMITOS CLR/FAST

RACE 7 POST 0122   RACE 8
PEPOE ESTATE 121   HEZANICECOAT
N BURGESS 120   J CREAGER 124
VICKIOUS SEC   BOB B PUMP
J YORKUN   121   D SMITH   124
CHICKSBRTH   DESKO FIRST DASH
J LEWIS   124   J LAMBERT 119
LARGE ANIMAL RACER   RENALT WEAPON
M MARS   124   G EIDE   119
EXECUTIVE KEY   IRISH EFFORT
R FIGUEROA 124   G BORG   119
MOTHER KAREN (L)   LUIGIS LEGEND
P SANCHEZ 122   G BORG   119
DUENDE MANTE   ANGRY ANGEL
O MONROY   124   R FIGUEROA 124
MISS MATH   EL MONTEHER
D STIMPSON 121   D MONTEHER 120
HAZZIN KATIE   KEEN DANCER (L)
R SEVILLE 121   J BADILLA 124
FIRST CHIC COPY   SILVER LINK
J CREAGER 124   J FUENTES 122
TAMMYS ALIBI   BRIGHTER BROTHER
R FIGUEROA 121   J FUENTES 124
                        KEY TO HIM
                        R PFAU   119

RACE 9
SHESIDEALFIGUREACUT
J CREAGER 124
CHIP IT
G SMITH   124
V LAMBERT 119
A GARCIA   124
LUIGIS LEGEND
G BORG   119
ANGRY ANGEL
R MARS   124
KEEN DANCER (L)
J BADILLA 124
K DIDERICK 124
D GLADNEY 124

RACE 10
PRA REFLECTION
M BURGESS 120
BIG RED QUIK
CR EMERALD (L)
CR VALERIE (L)
G EIDE   117
STURMI TERI
R PFAU   117
OH DESERT SHIELD
H SCHWERTS 115
A PULIDO   120
KITSON
P SANCHEZ 117
ROCKES BUICK PICK
J FUENTES 117
BAM ROSE
A WEINBERG 120

RACE 11
WIZARDOS LYNN
E GARCIA   124
J CREAGER 124
JAMES ARE FUN
O MONROY   124
LADY CHURCHILL
J BADILLA 124
EMMY RESULTS
A BAUTISTA 124
SHAKIN LOOSE
K DIDERICK 124

RACE 12
CHAIRMANS CHOICE
G BOAG   121
S TREASURE 121
SHED GOTTA LOOK
WHATS UP CHICK
R FIGUEROA 124
MISS POLVORIN DASH
J BADILLA 121
HIGH CLASS DASH
K DIDERICK 124
KARDHYN KUTIE
J LEWIS   124
WILMOTH
J MEIER   124
HONOLULU BUG
E GARCIA   124

WELCOME TO THE MIR

950 YDS GTR   4 1/2 FURLONGS   950 YDS GTR   4 1/2 FURLONGS   950 YDS G:R
3YO (MDN CLM)   3YO&UP (MDN CLM) 3YO&UP (ALW) FEM 3YO&UP (MDN ARAB) FEM 3YO&UP (CLM) &SEM

Hordes of sports bettors (left) crowd a NASA-esque race and sports book. Watching boxing, baseball, and horseracing at a casino is the next best thing to being at the arena, ballpark or track. Among other perks—parking is free! The "board," (below) which displays the information bettors need to place their wagers, is the focal point of a sports book. This baseball board lists the bet's reference number, the team, the day's listed pitcher, and the "line" (or odds).

Michael Coyne

BET#	NATIONAL LEAGUE – SATURDAY, JU		LINE	123
	TEAM	PITCHER		
EVEN	PHILLIES	QUANTRILL		132
–110	CARDS	K HILL		010
903	PIRATES	ERICKS	+165	8.5
904	EXPOS	C PEREZ	–175	
905	MARLINS	HAMMOND	+143	8.5
906	REDS	SCHOUREK	–153	
907	METS	MLICKI	+170	8.5
908	BRAVES	SMOLTZ	–180	
909	CUBS	FOSTER	+129	8.5
910	ASTROS	KILE	–139	
911	GIANTS	M LEITER	+172	7.5
912	DODGERS	NOMO	–182	
913	ROCKIES	RITZ	+133	8
914	PADRES	HAMILTON	–143	
BET#	AMERICAN LEAGUE – SATURDAY,		LINE	12
	TEAM	PITCHER		
+144	BLUE JAYS	JU GUZMAN		01
–154	YANKEES	M PEREZ		00
917	RED SOX	WAKEFIELD	–130	9
918	ORIOLES	KLINGENBEC	+120	
919	INDIANS	BLACK	–110	9
920	WHITE SOX	A FERNANDE	EVEN	
921	BREWERS	GIVENS	+110	10
922	TIGERS	MOORE	–120	
923	TWINS	ERICKSON	+145	8
924	ROYALS	GUBICZA	–155	
925	A'S	DARLING	+135	10
926	RANGERS	PAVLIK	–145	
927	ANGELS	FINLEY	+135	
928	MARINERS	JOHNSON	–145	

A B O V E

At the Rio Casino, you can play video-poker and watch your favorite soap opera at the same time.

Rick Browne

R I G H T

Gilda Dumore, an 84-year-old Daytona Beach woman, puts her weight into pulling the handle of this "Big Bertha," or giant four-reel slot machine, at the entrance to the Lady Luck Casino in downtown Las Vegas.

Susan Biddle

Japanese-speaking dealers
conduct free gambling classes for
Japanese tour groups at the San
Remo Hotel-Casino.

Michael Yamashita

At the Las Vegas International
Dealer School, students stand at
blackjack tables for hours and
practice "pitching" cards.
Shuffle machines and multi-deck
shoes could spell the slow demise
of the hand-held deck.

Robert Holmes

Gold rings and watchbands and hundred dollar bills—dealers and bosses refer to this as "Las Vegas flash."

Neil Farrin

Slot machine computer chips are programmed to pay off randomly. Alesia Fite from Sandusky, Ohio, was in the right place at the right time.

Nevada Wier

Blackjack, also known as "21," is the most popular table game in the casino, and with good reason: it's easy to play, the casino advantage is low, and entertainment value and social interaction are high. Here, a group of friends from Santa Cruz, Calif., share a laugh with a personable dealer.

James Marshall

Baccarat players wager in the splendor of The Mirage's exclusive Salon Privé. The highest of high rollers often play in casinos within the casino, private parlors far from the hubbub of the main floor.

James Marshall

Paul Endy of Paul-Son Gaming Supplies displays a few items from his warehouse. They are the largest producers of casino chips in the world, and also make gaming equipment and furniture.

Paul Chesley

An artist at Paul-Son Gaming Supplies designs a Mike Tyson commemorative chip. Limited collectors' edition chips are created for big sporting and entertainment events, then released into the chip supplies of the sponsoring casino. Collectors can acquire them right at the games while they play.

Paul Chesley

A casino "soft-count" room. The machine sorts, totals, and bundles the bills. Armored cars deliver the cash to banks around town, which employ high-tech accounting systems to ensure the accuracy of the deposits. The banks then ship the cash to central vaults, where it's counted again and stored. Surplus currency (over and above the vaults' storage capacities) is transferred to Federal Reserve facilities in Los Angeles, then redistributed around the West according to cash needs. Presumably, some of these same bills make it back to casino soft-count rooms.

Michael Yamashita

RIGHT

A casino "hard-count" room. Al Nichols pours dollar slot tokens into hoppers to be weighed and totaled by auditor Steven Montgomery. As an alternative to earmuffs, some casinos are hiring hearing-impaired personnel to work in the deafening hard-count room.

Acey Harper

Moulin Rouge poker chips. Money quickly loses its value when it's turned into colored clay tokens; it becomes a tool of the trade, like film to a photographer. "The guy who invented gambling was bright," Big Julie Weintraub, a legendary junket master from New York, once said. "But the guy who invented the chip was a genius."

Jeffery Salter

Slot enthusiast Marilyn Mearns plays a dollar machine at the Golden Nugget, a favorite venue for the upscale slot crowd. The classy four-star resort boasts a smorgasbord of shiny golden slot machines that accept everything from nickels to hundred dollar tokens.

Rick Browne

Psychic Kaye Rose gives a reading at the Psychic Eye Book Shop, one of a chain of a dozen stores in California and Nevada. She discerned an Egyptian background in the spiritual lineage of this young woman.

Rick Browne

Marilyn's back, as local photographer Timothy Davis shoots a portrait of a family reunion at Treasure Island. The Monroe image was hand-painted on the silk dinner jacket.

James Marshall

Amateur magicians get together once a month to practice card tricks and share legerdemain at Darwin's Magic Club.

Robert Maass

Local ladies share afternoon tea and a Victorian ambiance at Tricia's Teas, in an antique mall just off the Strip. Dresses and costumes are provided for those who want to get into the spirit of things.

Robert Holmes

A tattoo artist from Doc's Las Vegas Tattoo Co. leaves a lasting impression on a customer, who laughingly captures the moment on tape. Doc's motto is "We do it right the first time," which, in this business, is important.

Robert Maass

A confectioner adds ingredients to a batch of chocolate butter creams at Ethel M Chocolates, America's premier maker of fine boxed chocolates. Tours of the factory run daily, with the big payoff coming at the end ... a free sample.

Michael Yamashita

The term "roll 'em" has nothing to do with dice at the Don Pablo Cigar Co., where all cigars are hand rolled from tobacco of Cuban seed.

Michael Yamashita

At Serge Wigs, Julie Chevalier models one of a dozen John Travolta-type hairpieces produced for the "Splash II" revue at the Riviera.

Claus Meyer

Look-alike Heidi Thompson "chers" a pose with, and for, delighted visitors to the Forum Shops at Caesars. Right, Marvin Nathan portrays a "queen-sized" Cher in the Riviera's campy female impersonator show "La Cage."

Acey Harper (above)
Claus Meyer (right)

PREVIOUS PAGES

Dancers prepare for their performance in the main room at a classy Strip cabaret. An equal opportunity employer, it also has a room where male dancers entertain female patrons.

Andy Levin

ABOVE

More subdued casino cocktail uniforms, more appropriate to the clientele, are worn by the waitresses at the Horseshoe.

Robert Maass

RIGHT

Statuesque showgirl in "Jubilee," the long-running extravaganza at Bally's, gets her crown of rhinestones adjusted just right. Much of the headgear worn on Las Vegas stages can weigh up to 25 pounds, as opposed to the skimpy G-strings, which weigh but a few ounces.

Nevada Wier

Burt Lancon and Cindy
Landry, featured skaters in the
Stardust's main show "Enter the
Night," get ready to take to the ice
for one of their ten performances
each week. Both members of the
duo own impressive figure-skating
credentials, including U.S. and
Canadian national titles, and a
U.S. Olympic team berth for
Burt. A whole new set of skating
skills had to be developed to
work the 15-by-30-foot patch of
ice used in the show.

Claus Meyer

An archaeological excavation at Tule Springs in northern Las Vegas Valley uncovered some of North America's oldest arrow and spearheads and scarred animal bones, indicating that Valeo Indians lived here as early as 11,000 B.C. An outpost of the Anasazi thrived in Las Vegas Valley from A.D. 850 until around 1050. From roughly 1200 to the present, the Las Vegas Band of the Southern Paiute have lived in this corner of the Mojave Desert. Here, the Paiute are pictured during a powwow at their reservation just north of the city and at a Helldorado Week Powwow.

Michael Coyne

PREVIOUS PAGES

Traditional Las Vegas dancer—Tropicana's "Folies Bergere" (left); Traditional Native American dancer—Helldorado's "Powwow" (right).

Robert Holmes (left) and Michael Coyne (right)

The rainbow hues of Red Rock, the blue sky and white clouds; nature's own show of color in the desert.

Galen Rowell

Ethel M Chocolate's two and one half acre cactus gardens, containing more than 350 varieties of cacti, succulents, and desert plants collected from around the world. Some varieties bloom year round, although peak season for the garden is springtime. For camera‑totin' tourists there's free chocolate next door.

Mike Yamashita

Only 45 minutes from Las Vegas on the upper slopes of Mt. Charleston is a small grove of bristlecone pines, some of which were seedlings over 5,000 years ago.

Galen Rowell

Bipedal bovine brings big beer barrel into brewery—this mural adorns the Holy Cow!, Las Vegas' only micro-brewery.

Alex Webb

These dangling dice could roll sevens for businesses in the vicinty of this strip bustop following completion of a new 1,500-room mega-resort that will surround the Stratosphere Tower.

Alex Webb

Nurse Minta Albietz looks on as Jonathan Backers places a stethoscope on the heart of Kimberly San Agustin in the pediatric playroom at Sunrise Hospital. The playroom, the only one of its kind in southern Nevada, provides a place for hospitalized children to play with hospital equipment, become comfortable with medical procedures, learn to cope with treatment, and proceed with the normal development of their social and peer interaction skills.

Susan Biddle

Proud mom Jacqueline Wesley bonds with her 10-hour-old son Arlander in a delivery room at University Medical Center's Home Birthing Center.

Michael Coyne

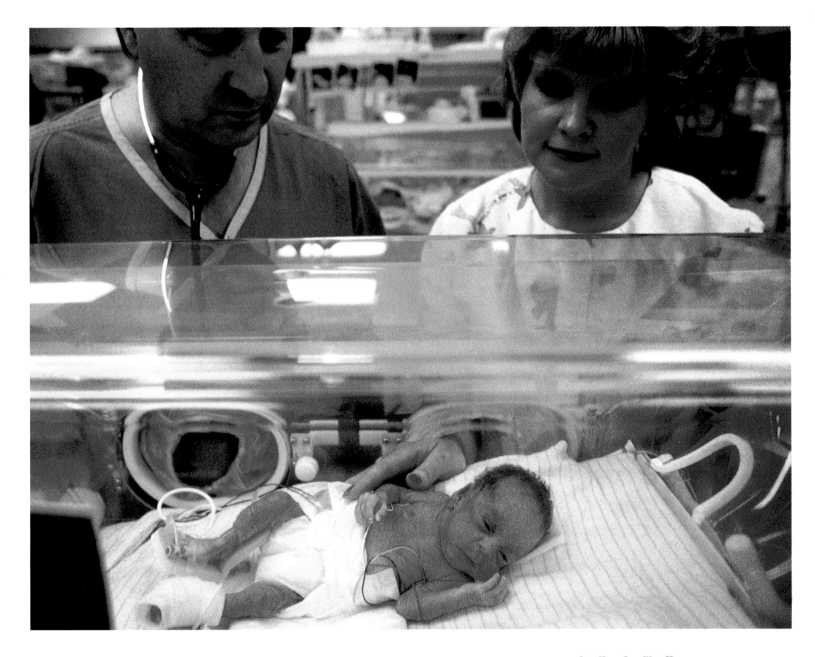

Preemie Cody Schell is safe, warm, and in the good hands of Dr. Rafael Zenteno and nurse Jennifer Hufano at Sunrise Hospital Neo-Natal, one of the finest neo-natal units in the western United States.

Susan Biddle

RIGHT

A popular way for families to spend a summer day is going to the ballpark to root for the Las Vegas Stars, the Triple A Minor league affiliate of the San Diego Padres. The small park and intimate atmosphere are refreshingly different from baseball as it's played today in most big-league parks.

Rick Browne

LEFT

S tars' third baseman Julio Bruno listens to the national anthem with a proud Brendan Cherr. Low admission prices, promotional days, and programs that bring the area's Little Leaguers together with the players have helped to endear the team to local fans for a decade.

James Marshall

A father's baseball lesson atop the action at Cashman Field. When it isn't hosting AAA baseball, the stadium serves as a venue for everything from swap meets to rock concerts.

James Marshall

Baseball and softball are big in Las Vegas, thanks to the cooperative climate, where the sun shines 300 days a year. (Right) A player for the Little Rascals hits a long fly ball in a T-ball game at Doolittle Community Center in North Las Vegas. (Below) Catcher Courtenay Thompson gives her Bobby Sox teammates a pep talk before the championship game of the Memorial Day Classic Tournament. Though they took second place in this tournament, they were the division champions the year before. (Left) Coach Victor Sanders watches his Little Rascals T-ball players, some of whom hope to follow in the footsteps of several home-town boys who made it big in the major leagues—most notably Cy Young Award winner Greg Maddux.

Jeffery Salter & James Marshall

Members of the Juliet Bike Racing Club, the only bicycle club in Las Vegas, work out on the road to Red Rock Canyon. The scenic 13-mile Red Rock Loop is a favorite, though challenging, bike ride only 15 miles from downtown.

Michael Coyne

A buckin' bronc tries to throw a rider at Helldorado, one of two big rodeos held in Las Vegas every year. The other is the National Finals Rodeo, considered the Super Bowl of rodeos.

Rick Browne

E xpansive Lake Mead, and the popular Black Canyon River, 30 miles east of the city center, are perfect for swimming, boating, jet skiing, fishing, even scuba diving.

Claus Meyer

A sphinx wannabe at Luxor.

Andy Levin

Pete Jagoda of Pete's Inflatables browses plaster statuettes imported from Tijuana at a swap meet in North Las Vegas.

Alex Webb

Poolercise? Nothing like water and sun to flesh out the fun in Las Vegas.

Michael Yamashita

Staying cool by the pool.

Jeff Gale

Tan lines at poolside.

Acey Harper

Atlantic bottlenose dolphins cruise the waters of their custom habitat at The Mirage. Rather than put these dolphins through paces in choreographed shows, the emphasis here is on education and observation.

Claus Meyer

Hot bodies, cool pool. For many, the Las Vegas sun has a stronger allure than even the fanciest casino.

Claus Meyer

Stakes are low, no one complains when drinks are spilled, and soggy bills are accepted without question at the Tropicana's famed swim-up blackjack table.

Robert Holmes

R I G H T

The pirate show at Treasure Island uses two 60-foot tall ships, 20 stuntmen, a booming sound system, and enough pyrotechnics to light up the Strip. A replica of the British Navy frigate, *Britannia*, sails into Buccaneer Bay and trades a few cannonballs with the pirate ship, *Hispaniola.* The navy then scores a direct hit on the pirates' cache of explosives (pictured here). The pirates answer, landing a knockout blow that sinks the *Britannia*, literally sending it to the bottom of the bay. It's eight minutes of swash-buckling, cannon-firing, powder-keg-exploding fun. And it's free.

Michael Coyne and James Marshall

P R E V I O U S
P A G E S

Poseidon's maintenance men? At Treasure Island's Buccaneer Bay divers effect underwater repairs on the mechanism that not only sails the British Navy's schooner, but sinks it on com-mand as well.

Acey Harper

Thousands of tiny lights reflect off the hood and windshield of a limousine leaving the portico of Jackie Gaughan's Plaza. The Plaza sits at the head of Fremont Street, which is nicknamed Glitter Gulch for its concentrated cumulus of blinking lights and neon.

Jeffery Salter

A healthy dose of glitter and gold adorns an elevator lobby at the MGM Grand. The MGM has 93 elevators in all, and its 30-story central elevator core is similar in size to a major city skyscraper.

Michael Yamashita

PREVIOUS PAGES

Of Las Vegas' nearly 90,000 hotel rooms, 15,000 of them occupy this corner, at Tropicana Avenue and the Strip, which also hosts 12,000 slot machines and nine showrooms. On a busy weekend, the 20,000 employees and 30,000 guests, along with innumerable players, diners, drinkers, showgoers, conventioneers, and gawkers make this four-corner neighborhood the third largest population center in all of Nevada, smaller than Reno but larger than Carson City, the state capital.

Rick Browne

ABOVE

Urban cowboy Tony Maragos of John Renton Lighting and Signs rides his bucket bronco to change burned-out lightbulbs in The Mirage's electronic readerboard.

Acey Harper

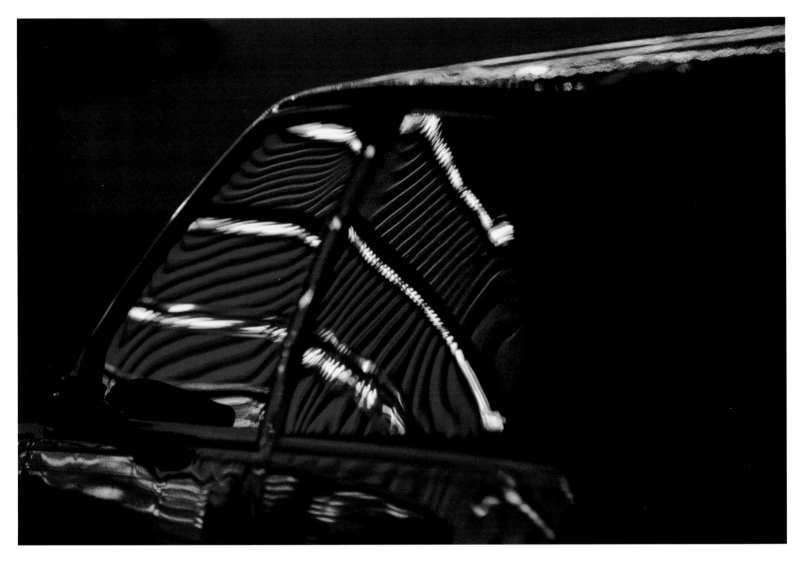

Bright ribbons of light reflect off cars parked near the famous quarter-mile long neon facade of the Stardust Hotel. Neon and argon are rare atmospheric gases that, when confined in a glass tube and zapped with high voltage, produce brilliant red and blue light. By painting the interior of the tubes with durable enamel, the entire spectrum can be achieved. The glass tubing is bent over Bunsen burners to create the complexity of curves. After dark, the signs come to life and the Strip blooms into an exotic garden of neon.

Acey Harper

Planet Vegas from the top of the Stratosphere Tower.

Paul Chesley

The stunning nine-story indoor park at Sam's Town is a glass-roofed cityscape that houses a forest, a rock waterfall, restaurants and bars, and synchonrized lasers and dancing waters featuring a howling wolf that steals the show.

Neil Farrin

Inside the great pyramid of Luxor, with a view of the largest atrium in the world. The second-floor houses a trilogy of high-tech-future entertainment "rides," which are produced using two motion simulators, large-screen high-resolution video, a stunning 3D segment, and an IMAX movie on a 70-foot tall screen.

Paul Chesley

A B O V E

Most high-roller suites, such as this one, cannot be rented for any price. They're reserved for the biggest players, people who have $100,000 credit lines, bet up to $2,000 a hand and, ironically, spend very little time in their rooms.

Nik Wheeler

R I G H T

The Forum Shops at Caesars is the most upscale shopping mall in the country. It has a cobble-stone floor, Roman statues, "al fresco" dining, and very high rents. The 92,000 feet of custom ceiling, designed by Sky Art of Colorado, undergoes a cycle controlled by a computer that changes the intensity of light from dawn to dusk in approximately one hour.

Michael Coyne

The bargain among bargains in Vegas is the $3 late-night steak at Binion's Horseshoe, shown here en route to the 450° grill. The eight-ounce New York strip steak, which comes with salad and baked potato, cost $2 for decades, but even at $3, you could order four or five of these for the price of one similar dinner at a hotel coffee shop in any other city in the country.

Robert Maass

Mary Rafalowski and John Neumiller hold "big food" items served at Billy Bob's Steakhouse at Sam's Town Hotel and Casino. An "onion blossom" appetizer, a Paul Bunyan 28-ounce ribeye, a half-pound sweet potato swathed in brown sugar and butter, a dinner salad the size of many chef's salads, a gallon of ice tea, one football-sized eclair, and their standard Mt. McKinley-sized, "slice" of chocolate cake.

Rick Browne

Thanks to the all-you-can-eat buffet, a quintessential Las Vegas experience, anyone with a few bucks and a loose belt can go for the gusto. Here, a cook grills meats and vegetables to order on the Mongolian barbecue at the Rio's sumptuous Carnival World Buffet.

Claus Meyer

Michelle McKinna, one of the Rio's "lpanema girls," voted the best cocktail waitresses in Las Vegas for each of the past five years by a reader's poll in the local newspaper.

Claus Meyer

ABOVE

The Arabian Nights segment from "EFX" at MGM Grand, the newest, hottest, and most technologically astounding extravaganza on the Las Vegas Strip this month.

Paul Chesley

RIGHT

Michael Crawford stands atop an enormous translucent sphere; just one of many high points of the MGM Grand's mega-production, "EFX." The merger of Broadway theater and Las Vegas spectacle bedazzles audiences with two firebreathing animatronic dragons, a spaceship, a time machine, and Crawford's unmistakable tenor.

Paul Chesley

Cirque du Soleil's "Mystère" at Treasure Island is perhaps the most popular show in Las Vegas—an eclectic combination of theater, dance, music, comedy, acrobatics, and new-age élan. François Dupuis, dressed up as an oversized baby, starts the show with a red rubber ball he "loses" in the unsuspecting audience.

Rick Browne

LEFT

The assembled ensemble at the end of one of Las Vegas' most memorable experiences—one reviewer called "Mystère" "the greatest, strangest show I've ever seen." It also was the inspiration for the title of this book.

Rick Browne

Gymnasts Christophe Suszek and Bogdan Zajac are painted green for their incredible gravity-defying balancing act performed on a revolving dome.

Rick Browne

Peggy the Clown at Circus Circus shares a quiet moment with some of the dozens of children she falls in love with every day.

Nevada Wier

The dedication of entertainers Siegfried and Roy in saving the white tiger species has led to the South African government asking the illusionists to save the white lions of Timbavati. Only eight white lions are known to exist on the planet. The one pictured, named Sarmoti, represents the beginning of Siegfried and Roy's quest to preserve the white lion species.

Michael Yamashita

Lance Burton's radiant personality and renowned close-up techniques have earned him countless accolades, including two Magician of the Year awards from the Academy of Magical Arts, and the prestigious World Champion Magician, from the Federation Internationale Sociétè de Magic. Burton recently signed a 13-year $100 million contract to create his own magic-theme extravaganza for the Monte Carlo mega-resort, a joint venture between The Mirage and Circus Circus.

Robert Holmes

RIGHT

In the local spirit of one-upmanship, Las Vegas jugglers have tossed everything from bowling balls to flaming torches, but Michael Goudeau of the Hacienda's "Lance Burton" show needs razor-sharp skills to handle these props.

Robert Holmes

And now for a little Liberace— "Liberace Play-A-Like" contest winner Victor Ngo tinkles tiny ivories at the most visited non-casino attraction in Las Vegas— the Liberace Museum. The museum is an absolute delight, filled with cars, pianos, elaborate costumes and other mementos of Mr. Showmanship's flamboyant life. And the Liberace Founda-tion quietly, and relentlessly, works in the background providing scholarships and grants to promising students interested in careers in the performing and creative arts.

Michael Coyne

The cast of "Starlight Express" joins in singing the finale. The Hilton added a giant ramp and runway to its showroom to accommodate the fast-paced roller-skating action of one of the most popular shows in town.

James Marshall

Ron Weber, who portrays "Greaseball," rejoices after winning his race in the Andrew Lloyd Webber musical "Starlight Express" at the Las Vegas Hilton. Cast members have to be in excellent condition to perform while wearing elaborate 50-pound train costumes, which cost between $10,000 and $20,000 apiece.

James Marshall

The Sun City Dancers perform at the Santa Fe Hotel & Casino three miles northwest of town. Las Vegas' most senior-friendly casino is also home to a full-size ice rink that's used for hockey games, exhibitions, Olympic training, and public skating.

Andy Levin

The Four Plaids star in "Forever Plaid," a quirky, clever, small-stage revue pulled off by four Perry Como-style crooners, two musicians, and little else. This modest production, which harkens back to the days of beatniks, Ozzie and Harriet, eight low-rise casinos on the Las Vegas Strip, and four-part guy groups like The Lettermen, has garnered a full complement of rave reviews.

Andy Levin

This venerable message of commiseration has been sympa-thizing with vanquished casino warriors since long before Excalibur (background) was a gleam in a builder's eye.

Paul Chesley

Police patrol downtown and the Strip on mountain bikes, which allow easy maneuvering through heavy traffic and access to sidewalks.

Paul Chesley

A pastoral scene in an older, quieter corner of America's fastest-growing and most glamorous city.

Paul Chesley

High profits from the casinos subsidize hotel food prices, which are used as loss leaders to attract people to play. But even non-casino neighborhood restaurants have to offer meal deals to compete for customers. The artist is not known.

Rick Browne

Legendary Las Vegas pioneer and Horseshoe hotel/casino founder Benny Binion, who was happiest on his Montana ranch, is immortalized here in bronze, atop a trusty steed. Benny appears to be pondering the changing Las Vegas landscape, with the steel framing for downtown's Fremont Street Experience peeking over the Horseshoe's roof from only a block away.

Alex Webb

R I G H T

Silver City, a small casino by Strip standards, markets to the value crowd with 99¢ breakfasts and $1-per-hand blackjack.

Claus Meyer

R I G H T

The "space frame" for the Fremont Street Experience is four blocks long, a hundred feet high, and incorporates two million lightbulbs. This "celestial vault" provides a dramatic foyer that unifies Fremont Street's 11 hotel-casinos.

Nik Wheeler

R I G H T

Even a red light doesn't stop the action on Las Vegas Boulevard.

James Marshall

R I G H T

Stunning Marilyn Monroe look-alike Bettina Best waits for a burger and fries at the popular, and take-you-back-a-few-years, Sonic drive-in in West Las Vegas. Her chariot: a Duesenberg from the Imperial Palace's Antique & Classic Auto Collection.

Robert Holmes

B E L O W

Jammin' on the Strip—traffic, people, buildings, and signs jam together in a city which hosts 29 million visitors a year, an average of 170,000 people per day.

Neil Farrin

L E F T

Nostalgia is a favorite and recurring theme in several of the Strip's song and dance revues. The hairdo of a cast member from "Beehive" is a made-to-order advertisement for the Sahara's set-in-the-'60s show which brings back "girl group" sounds as well as poodle skirts and sky-scrapin' coiffures.

Andy Levin

A B O V E

Sometimes clear, sometimes distorted, everyone has their own reflections on what is Las Vegas .

Michael Coyne

The riddle that this sphinx contemplates is Luxor, a dramatic departure from traditional Las Vegas hotel architecture. With 39,000 windows and the Nile River flowing inside, it's not your standard-issue pyramid,

Neil Farrin

After scaling the 350-foot side of the Luxor pyramid, photographer-climber Galen Rowell pauses at the pinnacle to survey the cityscape—hoping no one fires up the 40-billion-candlepower spotlight right below him.

Galen Rowell

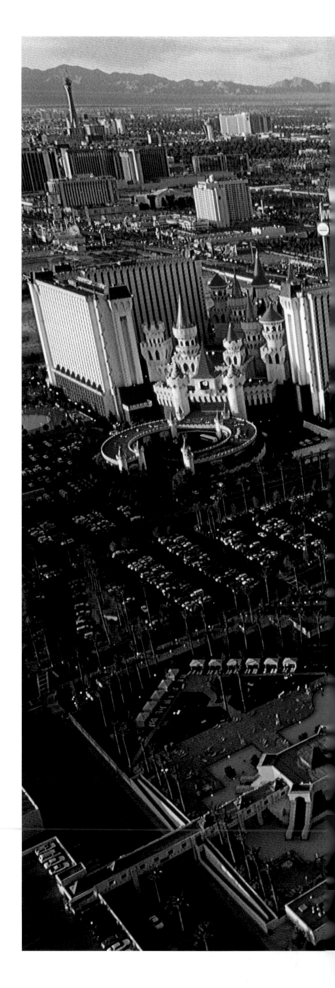

High-wire warriors work without a safety net at the 900-foot level of the Stratosphere Tower. The tower soars to 1,149 feet, making it the tallest structure west of the Mississippi. A roller coaster and zero-gravity ride, wedding chapels, high-roller suites, and a revolving restaurant and bar adorn the top.

Paul Chesley

Theme casinos are de rigueur in the '90s: Egyptian (Luxor), Arthurian (Excalibur), Polynesian (The Mirage), Buccaneer (Treasure Island), Mediterranean (the new Beau Rivage, to be built by Mirage Resorts), and Parisian (the new Paris, to be built by, and next to, Bally's). Other themes include the railroad (Palace and Boulder Stations), movies (MGM Grand), even Manhattan (New York, New York, to be built across from the MGM Grand).

Neil Farrin

173

The desert-sky-du-jour is a brilliant burnt orange as Mother Nature colors the sky before the man-made light show of the Strip hotels fires up the night.

Galen Rowell

LEFT

The Normandie Motel posts a clever display of self-promotion.

Neil Farrin

ABOVE

The oft-photographed Las Vegas welcome sign is just a rearview mirror memory on the drive out of town.

Alex Webb

A lone couple two-steps gently
into the night on the dance floor
of Wild Bill's Country Restaurant
dance floor, at the Excalibur,
oblivious to the fact that it's long
past closing time.

James Marshall

PHOTOGRAPHERS
Susan Biddle
Rick Browne
Paul Chesley
Michael Coyne
Neil Farrin
Jeff Gale
Acey Harper
Robert Holmes
Andy Levin

Robert Maass
James Marshall
Claus Meyer
Galen Rowell
Jeffery Allan Salter
Alex Webb
Nik Wheeler
Nevada Wier
Michael Yamashita

DIRECTORS
Rick Browne
James Marshall

INTRODUCTION
Kenny Rogers

DIRECTOR OF PHOTOGRAPHY
Michael Coyne

PICTURE EDITORS
Bill Black, *Travel Holiday*
Ron Meyerson, Ron Meyerson Designs
George Olson, Freelance

DESIGNER
Tom Morgan, Blue Design

CAPTIONS
Deke Castleman, *Las Vegas Advisor*
Anthony Curtis, *Las Vegas Advisor*

LOGISTICS COORDINATOR
Linda Lamb

ASSIGNMENT COORDINATOR
Barry Sundermeier

PUBLICISTS
Leslie Rossman, HarperCollins, SF
Don Payne, Don Payne Media Link

VIDEOGRAPHER
Norm Nusbaum, Goodwyn
Production Group

RESEARCH ASSOCIATE
Virginia Castleman

PRODUCTION ASSISTANTS
Chris Browne
Tom Eidsmore

Susan Biddle

Denver, Colorado

Susan Biddle is currently a freelance photographer covering assignments for various magazines, newspapers, and corporations including *Time*, *Life*, *National Geographic*, and *TheNew York Times*. She began her career at the Peace Corps where she became Director of Photography. She then worked as staff photographer for *The Topeka Capital-Journal* and *The Denver Post* and as a White House photographer during the last year of the Reagan administration, and the Bush administration. Susan has participated in several book projects including *A Day in the Life of America*, *Baseball in America*, *Hong Kong: Here be Dragons*, and *A Day in the Life of Thailand*.

Rick Browne—*Planet Vegas Co-Director*

Scotts Valley, California

Rick Browne is an internationally known writer and photojournalist whose assignments span the globe. Having traveled extensively for major magazines and corporate clients, he specializes in Pacific Rim and European countries. His work is regularly featured in a wide variety of domestic and foreign magazines including *People*, *The Los Angeles Times*, *Time*, *Newsweek*, *Burda*, *Travel & Leisure*, and *TravelAge West*. He recently received the silver medal from the Society of American Travel Writers for his travel photography. Co-founder of Pacific Rim Concepts he also was co-director and contributing photographer to *A Day in the Life of Thailand*, director and co-editor of the book *Hong Kong: Here be Dragons* and a contributing photographer to both *A Day in the Life of Israel* and *Jerusalem 3000*.

Paul Chesley

Aspen, Colorado

Paul Chesley has been a freelance photographer with *National Geographic* since 1975, and has completed over 35 projects worldwide with the Society. He was recently honored by the inclusion of his work in the Society's first major exhibition "The Art of Photography at National Geographic: A 100 Year Retrospective" at the Corcoran Gallery of Art in Washington, D.C. Solo exhibitions of his work have appeared in museums in London, Tokyo, New York, and Honolulu. His greatest enjoyment is on international projects, capturing the lives of the people, the culture, and beauty of Asia and the South Pacific. He has been a regular contributor to the renowned series, *A Day in the Life*, and his photographic essays are frequently featured in magazines including *Life*, *Fortune*, *GEO*, *Newsweek*, and *Time*.

Michael Coyne

Sydney, Australia

Michael Coyne worked for eight years covering the Iranian revolution during which time his work appeared in magazines such as *Newsweek*, *Life*, *Time*, *German Geo*, *London Observer*, and included a 28-page spread in *National Geographic*.

His two very successful books on Australia, *The Oz Factor* and *A World of Australians*, have resulted in national and international awards. For his work in the Middle East he has received many awards, including those from the National Press Photographers Association and the Overseas Press Club of America. In 1995 he was honored as the "Magazine Photographer of the Year" in Australia.

Neil Farrin

Hong Kong

Neil Farrin arrived in Hong Kong in 1977, having spent five years working primarily as a photojournalist for the UK press, at the *Times*, and *Telegraph*. The last 15 years have taken him on assignment to Scotland, Germany, Sweden, Australia, New Zealand, Southeast Asia, and the United States. His photography includes annual reports, corporate brochures, and advertising campaigns and his journalistic work appears in *GEO*, *Time*, *Newsweek*, and *The Sunday Times*. Farrin was a contributor to the books *Hong Kong: Here be Dragons* and *A Day in the Life of Thailand*. He currently runs Pro-File Photo Library in Hong Kong and Singapore.

Jeff Gale

Las Vegas, Nevada

Jeff Gale graduated from North Texas State University. He moved to Las Vegas in the late 70s to pursue his career as a commercial photographer. Las Vegas was a prime city for Jeff, where he created nationally recognized work for major strip hotels and casinos, manufacturing plants, and financial institutions across the southwest. After being in the commercial photography business for 10 years, Jeff teamed up with business partner Sheri Shelton to open what is now the leading commercial lab and imaging plant in Nevada, Photo Finish. Photo Finish has established itself as one of the finest facilities in the country for processing, printing, and digital imaging. Photo Finish has been in business since 1984. Jeff is president and chief photographer for the company.

Acey Harper

Tiburon, California

Acey Harper, whose work was recently selected for the cover of *A Day in the Life of Israel*, works as a freelance photographer and picture editor based out of Tiburon, California. He has traveled worldwide for such clients as *People*, *National Geographic*, and *USA Today* and is currently managing director of the photo agency, Reportage Stock. Most recently, Harper served as the director of photography for *The Mission: Inside the Church of Latter-day Saints*.

Robert Holmes

Mill Valley, California

British photographer Robert Holmes, who was invited to the United States by Ansel Adams, embarked on a distinguished career in editorial photography covering the 1975 British Everest Expedition for *Paris Match*, *Stern*, and the London *Daily Mail*. Since then, Holmes has traveled throughout the world on assignment for most of the world's major travel magazines, including *National Geographic*, *Geo*, *Travel & Leisure*, *Islands*, and *Departures*. Holmes has 15 books in print and is both author and photographer of *The Thomas Cook Guides* to California, Boston & New England, and Hawaii. He was the recipient of the coveted Travel Photographer of the Year award from the Society of American Travel Writers in 1990 and in 1992.

Andy Levin

New York, New York

Andy Levin is a contributing photographer at *Life* magazine and a frequent contributor to *People* magazine. He is a veteran of ten *Day in the Life* books, including *A Day in the Life of Canada*, *A Day in the Life of America*, *A Day in the Life of Italy*, and *A Day in the Life of Ireland*. A former POY photo essay winner, his personal work was featured in a recent cover story in the British photojournalist review *Reportage*. Levin is currently working on a long-term project dealing with beach culture from Bombay to Coney Island.

The Clubhouse Tavern, where local bikers recently raised thousands of dollars to help a five-year-old Las Vegas child with leukemia. Paul Chesley

Robin Miller, lead dancer in Hot Rock N Country at the Plaza, in the casino after the Show.   Bill Black

Robert Maass

New York, New York

Currently under contract with *Newsweek* as a contributing photographer, Robert Maass has been working as a freelance photographer since 1980. His work has been published in a large variety of domestic and international publications, covering assignments in the United States, east and west Europe, the Soviet Union, the Indian subcontinent, Asia, east Africa and Nicaragua. In 1989 and 1991, Maass covered famine relief efforts in southern Sudan. In 1989 and 1990 he covered the revolutions in Czechoslovakia and Romania. Maass has written and photographed six children's books and was a contributor to *Baseball in America* and *Hong Kong: Here be Dragons.*

James Marshall—*Planet Vegas Co-Director*

New York, New York

James Marshall began photography in a basement darkroom at age 15, and has retained a fascination for the power of visual imagery ever since. He received an MFA from Pratt Institute in New York City, and has since spent many years traveling extensively in Asia and Europe, contributing photography to numerous international publications including *The New York Times, Newsweek, Travel & Leisure, Geo* and *Smithsonian.* Cofounder of Pacific Rim Concepts, a book packaging company specializing in fine photographic books, he produced and co-edited *Hong Kong: Here be Dragons* and was co-director and photographer for *A Day in the Life of Thailand.* He is also a contributing photographer to *A Day in the Life of Israel* and *Jerusalem 3000.*

Claus Meyer

Rio de Janeiro, Brazil

The winner of many prizes and awards, Claus Meyer was selected in 1985 by Communication World as one of the top annual report photographers in the world. His excellence in color photography has been recognized by Kodak and Nikon, and in 1981 he won a Nikon International Grand Prize. He has published several books on Brazil, most recently a book on the Amazon. Claus is one of the few photographers who participated on all fourteen titles of the *Day in the Life* series.

Galen Rowell

Albany, California

Galen Rowell is a photographer and writer specializing in nature and adventure. He has done 12 large-format photography books and many articles for *National Geographic.* His monthly column appears in *Outdoor Photographer,* and his most recent work has involved over 20 trips to the Arctic and Antarctic for his fall 1995 book, *Poles Apart.* In 1984 he received the Ansel Adams Award for wilderness photography, and in 1992 a National Science Foundation Grant to photograph Antarctica. His work has been widely exhibited in such galleries as Nikon House, the International Center of Photography, and the Smithsonian Institute.

Jeffery Allan Salter

Miami, Florida

In high school, his classmates called him the cameraman. Now they know him as Jeffery A. Salter, the award-winning photojournalist who has covered such global events as the bombing of Pan Am 108 over the skies of Lockerbie, Scotland, and the deadly Haitian democracy elections of November 1987. Currently Salter is a staff photographer with *The Miami Herald.* Previously he worked for *Newsday, The Bergen Record, The Virginian Pilot/Ledger Star,* and *Navy Times.* Salter has won numerous awards and was New Jersey Photographer of the Year. His work has appeared in *The African Americans, Songs of My People, A Day in the Life of Israel,* and *A Day in the Life of Thailand.*

Alex Webb

New York, New York

Born in San Francisco, Alex Webb has been working as a photojournalist since 1974, joining Magnum Photos as an associate member in 1976. His work has appeared in *Life, The New York Times Magazine, Geo,* and *National Geographic.* Traveling through Mexico, the Caribbean, Latin America, and Africa, Webb published two books, *Hot Light/Half-Made Worlds: Photographs from the Tropics* and *Under a Grudging Sun: Photographs from Haiti Libere 1986-1988.* In 1993 he spent much of the year photographing the Amazon river, from mouth to source, and in 1994 was a contributing photographer to *A Day in the Life of Thailand.* He is currently working on a book of his work from Florida.

Nik Wheeler

Los Angeles, California

Born in Hitchin, England, Nik Wheeler attended the local high school and later studied French and Drama at Bristol University and French Civilization at the Sorbonne, Paris. Starting his photographic career in Bangkok, he moved to Vietnam as a combat photographer and covered the Tet Offensive. In 1970 he went to the Middle East working out of Beirut, and covered the Jordan Civil War for *Time,* the October War for *Newsweek,* and did assignments for *National Geographic* and *Paris Match.* Currently living in Los Angeles, he covers assignments for *National Geographic, Geo, Travel & Leisure,* and *Travel Holiday.* Published books include *Return to the Marshes, Iraq—Land of Two Rivers, This is China,* and *Cloud Dwellers of the Himalayas.* In 1988, he was named Photographer of the Year by the Society of American Travel Writers. Most recently his work appears in *A Day in the Life of Israel* and *A Day in the Life of Thailand.*

Nevada Wier

Santa Fe, New Mexico

Nevada Wier is a photographer specializing in the remote corners of the globe, particularly Asia. She is a Fellow of The Explorer's Club and a photographer with The Image Bank. Her work has been published in numerous national and international publications including: *Outdoor Photographer, Smithsonian, Natural History, Popular Photography, Outside, Sawasdee, Photo Asia,* and *Discovery.* Nevada is also a contributing editor and photography columnist for *Escape,* a new adventure travel magazine. Nevada's recent book, *The Land of Nine Dragons —Vietnam Today,* won the Lowell Thomas Best Travel Book of 1992 award. She was a participating photographer in *A Day in the Life of Thailand.* Nevada is currently working on *A Nomadic Life,* a book on the Kirghiz people in the Pamir mountains of western China, to be published in 1997.

Michael Yamashita

Mendham, New Jersey

Photographer Michael Yamashita started taking pictures while on a "roots" trip to Japan in 1971. What began as a hobby led to a career that has taken him to six continents and combined his two passions — photography and travel. Yamashita's work for *National Geographic* has included such wide-ranging locations as Somalia and Sudan, England, Ireland, New Guinea, New Jersey, and Japan. He has published two books, *The Mekong: Mother of Waters* and *In the Japanese Garden;* the latter received numerous awards, including three from the Garden Writers of America. Yamashita has participated in four *Day in the Life* book projects and has received awards from a variety of professional organizations including the National Press Photographers Association Pictures of the Year competition. His work has been displayed at the National Gallery of Art, the Los Angeles County Museum of Art, and Kodak's Professional Photographer's Showcase at Epcot Center.

Las Vegas Convention & Visitors Authority

The Nevada Legislature created the Clark County Fair and Recreation Board in 1955 which evolved into the current world-recognized and award-winning Las Vegas Convention and Visitors Authority. The LVCVA is governed by a 12-member board including seven elected city and county officials and five members representing private industry. The LVCVA not only operates and maintains the Las Vegas Convention Center near the Strip, and its satellite multi-purpose Cashman Field Center near downtown Las Vegas, but plays a major role in marketing Las Vegas as a worldwide resort and convention destination for domestic and international travelers. Initial construction of the Convention Center began in 1957 and required 18 months to complete.

In less than four decades, with additional projects on the drawing board, the center expanded into one of the largest single-story facilities in the world with 1.6 million square feet of meeting and convention space. By the time Las Vegas celebrated its 90th birthday in 1995, more than one million people lived in the Las Vegas metropolitan area. That same year, LVCVA estimated more than 29 million travelers from throughout the world visited Las Vegas, where Lady Luck and her imaginative entrepreneurs had wagered fortunes on the future—and won. The once tiny railroad town had become the largest U.S. city born in the 20th century and Las Vegas was voted the World's Best Gaming Destination by a quarter-million worldwide travel companies.

Mirage Resorts Inc.

Many credit Mirage Resorts, Incorporated with the creation of a "new" Las Vegas. In fact, the 1989 opening of The Mirage can be seen historically as the beginning of a major repositioning of Las Vegas as a world-class destination resort. It also marked the beginning of a building boom which has seen more than $5 billion invested in the Las Vegas gaming market during a five-year period with billions more on the horizon.

Mirage Resorts owns and operates the Golden Nugget in downtown Las Vegas, The Mirage and Treasure Island on the Las Vegas "Strip" and the Golden Nugget in Laughlin, Nevada. This company, which began as a small casino on Fremont Street in 1946, is now a $3 billion company with a family of employees topping 18,000. Mirage Resorts' future plans call for the creation of a dynamic new resort for development on the site of the historic Dunes hotel. This resort, which promises to be the most romantic in the world, is positioned to lead Las Vegas into the next century.

Landmark Entertainment Group

Landmark Entertainment Group is the world's leading designer of theme parks and theme park attractions. The Landmark touch can be seen in many of the world's leading theme parks including Universal Studios Hollywood, Universal Studios Florida, Busch Gardens, Six Flags Over Georgia, Six Flags Astroworld, and Sanrio Puroland. As designers of some of the world's largest and most spectacular attractions, Landmark has pioneered the merging of technology and design to create stunning new entertainment experiences.

Beginning in 1985, Landmark began its association with Las Vegas by pioneering "entertainment architecture" for casino clients that included Caesars Palace, ITT Sheraton and Harrah's. Landmark's many designs have become true Las Vegas "landmarks" and are among the most popular, and most-photographed locations in the city. Landmark continues to expand upon its relationship with Las Vegas and is currently creating new visions for the Las Vegas of the next century. As one of the key firms responsible for reinventing Las Vegas in the 90's, Landmark is proud to sponsor this spectacular commemorative book on what is perhaps, the most exciting city for entertainment in the world.

Ethel M Chocolates, Inc.

Renowned chocolatier Forrest Mars had a vision—to create premium chocolates so exquisite in taste and appearance that they would be regarded as the most genuine expression of affection that one could give or receive. He brought that vision to life with the founding of Ethel M Chocolates in Las Vegas in 1981. Since then, Ethel M associates have been dedicated to the creation of unique and inspired chocolates. Using only the finest ingredients, they create extraordinary chocolates such as the legendary lemon buttercreams, elegant cream liqueurs and irresitible ALMOND BUTTER KRISPS™ confections.

The self-guided factory tour is a delight for the senses with a view of the chocolate-making process and free chocolate sampling. A rock-lined pathway leads visitors through the adjacent world-class cactus garden exhibiting 350 varieties of shrubs, succulents and cacti. Complete the tour of the Ethel M facility with a stop at the state of the art environmentally-friendly water recycling plant.

First Interstate Bank of Nevada

With offices throughout Southern Nevada, First Interstate Bank is closely connected to the mosaic of people and cultures that make up greater Las Vegas. Through a variety of ways, we are active in the diverse communities we serve.

Our employees read to elementary school students, deliver presents to nursing home seniors and throw birthday parties for abused children. They donated about 50,000 hours of community service last year in Southern Nevada and First Interstate contributed more than $600,000 to community activities here.

First Interstate serves the banking needs of third graders opening their first savings accounts, start-up businesses in minority neighborhoods and corporate resorts, among many others; and we are proud to say that our rich mixture of customers statewide have entrusted us with $3.4 billion in deposits.

Howard Hughes Corporation

The Howard Hughes Corporation, the operating arm of the Howard R. Hughes Estate, currently owns more than 21,000 acres of land acquired by Hughes and is involved exclusively in real estate investment and development. The company, which has targeted its development plans to properties in Southern Nevada and Southern California, incorporates the spirit of Hughes' vision and business acumen in all aspects of the company's residential, commercial and industrial developments.

The Howard Hughes Corporation's holdings include: 20,000 acres in the 22,500-acre master-planned community of Summerlin, the best selling community in the country; The Crossing Business Center, a 115-acre business park and employment center located within Summerlin; Hughes Center, a 120-acre master-planned mixed-use business center located in the high growth area of central Las Vegas; Hughes Airport Center, a 390-acre master-planned business and industrial park located south of McCarran International Airport; Hughes Cheyenne Center, a 209-acre master-planned industrial park located in North Las Vegas; Howard Hughes Center, a 70-acre institutional-quality master-planned mixed-use development in West Los Angeles; and Playa Vista, a 1,087-acre mixed-use community in West Los Angeles being developed in a joint venture with Maguire Thomas Partners.

Nevada Power Company.

When Nevada Power Company began serving the Las Vegas area in 1906, a single power line lit up downtown Las Vegas. Today, 89 years later, Nevada Power's 11,000 miles of power lines keep the world famous "Lights of Las Vegas" on and provide power to its one million residents. Meeting the electric needs of this dynamic community is a formidable challenge, but not the only challenge Nevada Power faces. Like other electric utilities across the nation, we too have been racing the pace of change in the electric industry.

While connecting service to as many as 6,000 new customers a month, Nevada Power has set its sights on the future. We have equipped ourselves to meet a future that holds continued growth for our service territory and increased competition in the industry. We embrace these new changes as we continue our role as a leader in the electric utility industry. Additionally, Nevada Power is proud to be a corporate and environmental leader in the community. We encourage and support employee volunteerism and take pride in building effective partnerships with the communities we serve.

Photo Finish Custom Color Lab

Photo Finish, a custom photo lab and digital imaging service located in Las Vegas, took great pride in being selected as the processing plant for the 1,500 rolls of film shot for the *Planet Vegas* book. For over a decade, Photo Finish has been the custom photo lab preferred by photographers, designers, architects, builders, advertising agencies and major corporate clients.

Supplying wallet-size to wall-size photographs, consistent accurate duplicating services, and state of the art digital imaging services, Photo Finish has been recognized as a Kodak Q-Lab as a leader in the field of photofinishing and digital imaging. Our technicians and management are dedicated to artists of all kinds around the world. "Our Business is to make Your Business Look Good."

Paul-Son Gaming Supplies

Paul-Son is the leading manufacturer and supplier of casino equipment in the United States. The company was founded in 1963 by its current chairman, Paul S. Endy. Their products include casino chips, table layouts, playing cards, dice, gaming furniture and miscellaneous table accessories used in table games such as blackjack, poker, baccarat, craps and roulette.

The company is headquartered in Las Vegas, Nevada, with manufacturing facilities located in Las Vegas and San Luis, Mexico. Sales offices are in Las Vegas, Reno, Atlantic City, Gulfport Mississippi, New Orleans, California and Canada. The company sells its products in every state in which casinos operate and enjoys 75% - 80% of the market share in the United States. As the international market continues to grow, Paul-Son has established distributors in an additional 26 countries through London Casino Supplies of London.

Calypso Imaging

Located in the heart of California's Silicon Valley, Calypso draws its resources from its surrounding environment. The Silicon Valley has provided fertile ground for many of the best ideas and achievements of the digital revolution. For twenty-three years Calypso Imaging has provided the imaging needs of industry and the arts and honed its skills on the hard rock of market demands.

Today, Calypso Imaging blends the craftsmanship of the traditional photographic lab with the best of digital technology. Calypso Imaging is

uniquely qualified to offer technically expert, one-on-one, full service project management from concept through completion for designers, photographers and professionals from all industries and all parts of the globe.

Reno Air

Reno Air is a Nevada-based national air carrier which provides low cost, full service scheduled air transportation for passengers, freight and mail. Reno Air serves many cities throughout the West, including Las Vegas, San Jose, San Diego, Los Angeles, Orange County, Seattle, Portland, Tucson, Colorado Springs, Vancouver, B.C., and its hometown of Reno/Tahoe. The carrier currently operates McDonnell Douglas MD-80 series jets with an average age of four years, and offers its customers assigned seating, advanced boarding passes and a first class cabin. Reno Air is a participating carrier in the American Airlines AAdvantage Travel Awards Program, and fully participates in all travel agency reservations systems.

The Rio Suite Hotel & Casino

Service, service, service. These are the words that clearly describe the promised experience to every guest who walks through the Rio's doors ... period. Since our inception in 1990 as the only all suite hotel and casino in the world, we have added two towers and an unbelievable array of experiences. We now stand poised for future expansions with 1,410 rooms to date.

Currently the Rio is nationally recognized by the 1995 Zagat Survey of U.S. Hotels , Resorts, and Spas as the best overall hotel/casino Las Vegas has to offer. We boast Las Vegas' most innovative dining experiences, a gorgeous waterfall beach—home to special concert events, and an endless variety of table games and slots. Our multimillion dollar Copacabana Entertainment complex is home to the sensuous Copacabana Dinner Show and America's hottest video nightclub . . . Club Rio. Located on I-15 and West Flamingo, one mile west of the Strip, The Rio is a complete Las Vegas vacation destination, now. . . and for the future.

Sunrise Hospital and Medical Center

Sunrise Hospital and Medical Center and Sunrise Children's Hospital combine to create the largest comprehensive medical complex in Nevada with 688 beds. Serving Las Vegans and residents in surrounding communities for more than 35 years, Sunrise has been instrumental in bringing the most qualified healthcare professionals and the newest medical technology to Southern Nevada. The JCAHO-accredited facility is recognized as a leading force in developing innovative and alternative healthcare programs.

The Sunrise name and standard of care is

associated with several medical facilities throughout the rapidly growing Las Vegas Valley, combining to provide Southern Nevadans with a complete system of healthcare delivery. The $25 million expansion and renovation of Sunrise's new state-of-the-art surgical center will be completed in the Fall, and the new Sunrise Mountain View Hospital and Medical Center, a $65 million, 215,000-square-foot medical center in northwest Las Vegas, is scheduled to open in early 1996.

Value Rent-A-Car

To provide easier access to business and leisure travelers, Value Rent-A-Car offers two locations in Las Vegas. Servicing McCarran International Airport on Paradise Road and at the Fitzgerald Hotel on Fremont Street, Value features the best of the Mitsubishi line, including the Diamante luxury performance sedan and the Galant family sedan. Value offers free unlimited mileage and free area pick-ups.

Value Rent-A-Car, Inc., is a subsidiary of Mitsubishi Motor Sales of America, Inc. Value operates in almost 50 locations throughout the United States with 33 locations in Florida. Now in-airport in eight cities—Atlanta, Daytona Beach, Denver, Fort Myers, Miami, Sarasota, Tucson and West Palm Beach—Value has a fleet of more than 25,000 vehicles, offering a wide variety of domestic and imported rental cars. Value features the Mitsubishi Diamante luxury performance sedan, Galant family sedan and Expo sport wagon, as well as the Dodge Caravan and the Chrysler New Yorker and LeBaron convertible.

Sundance Helicopters

Sundance Helicopters is the oldest and largest helicopter company in Las Vegas and the State of Nevada. Founded over a decade ago, Sundance has won awards for excellence in its safety record and for customer service.

A full-service helicopter company, Sundance Helicopters is a reflection of the great diversity of activities in and around Las Vegas itself. While tours to the Grand Canyon and other area attractions are a leading market, Sundance provides services for wide variety of uses on a charter basis including aerial photography, VIP transport, construction lift, night sky sign advertising, news gathering, and natural resource management.

Picture Pocket Corp.

Picture Pocket Corp. is a worldwide manufacturer of film preservation products. Our line of film sleeves has become the choice of thousands of professional labs from around the world. The producers of this book used our Heavy Duty Slide Album pages to organize, view and select their shots.

Thanks to . . .

Unlike the rest of our solar system, Planet Vegas didn't just explode into the cosmos with a big bang. This book came about because lots of extraordinary people cared, worked very hard, and put their hearts and minds into helping two guys with a dream create something special.

The following pages list the names and affiliations of many of those who helped make this project work, and to these magical people, as well as any we have missed, we give our sincerest thanks and our deepest gratitude.

We literally couldn't have done it without you.

Rick & Jim
June 28, 1995

Underwriters

Las Vegas Convention and Visitors Authority
Mirage Resorts, Incorporated
Landmark Entertainment Group

Sponsors

Calypso Imaging
Eastman Kodak Company
Ethel M Chocolates, Inc.
First Interstate Bank
Howard Hughes Corporation
Nevada Power Company
Paul-Son Gaming Supplies
Photo Finish Color Lab
Picture Pocket Corporation
Reno Air
Rio Suite Hotel & Casino
Sundance Helicopters
Sunrise Hospital & Medical Center
Value Rent-A-Car

Contributors & friends

Peter Aaronson, Bally's
Deb & Bob Abendrothe
Judy Acevedo
Harry Akoopie
Leonardo Alarcon
Rick Allen, Eastman Kodak
Richard Amalfitano, Golden Nugget
Patricia Ambrose, Landmark Entertainment
Lisa Amerson, Aladdin
Doug Andrews, Nevada Printing
Kathy & John Angood
Tim Apple, Treasure Island
Joan Armstrong
Charlene Ashfield, Scotts Valley Rec. Dept.
Timothy B. Davis
John Bachmann
Treasure Bailley
Bobbi Baker Burroughs, LIFE Magazine
Bobby Baldwin, Mirage Resorts, Inc.
Anthony Barelli, MD
Kay Barnes
Jenny Barry, Collins San Francisco
Scott Batdorff, Calypso Imaging
The Beach Boys
Pat Bechelli
Bee Engineering
Koby Bennett
Robert Benz, HMI
Richard Berkvam
Tina Best
Carole Bidnick, Collins San Francisco
Kish Big Cat, Rainbow Shield Singers

Trent Billingsley
Marj Binette, ROGO Productions
Benny Binion
Jack Binion
Suzi Black
Brenda Boivin
Sonny Boline
Bobby Boling, Legends in Concert
Myram Borders, LVCVA News Bureau
Kathryn Boschetto
Cynthia Bosher
Dorothy Bowen
Loretta Bowman
William Boyd
Dan Bradley, Wet 'n Wild
Aileen Brodsky, Treasure Island
Doug Brooks
John Brooks
Mark Brown, Howard Hughes Corp.
Kathleen Browne
Dorothy Browne
Kara Browne
Tricia Browne
Grant & June Browne
Bob & Marti Browne
Tom Bruny
Warren Burr, Loomis
Nathan Burr, Treasure Island
Darrin Bush, The Righteous Brothers
Anne & Terry Callon
Gary Campbell, Backstage
Kathilynn Carpenter, Fremont Street Experience
Tim Cashman, Cashman Cadillac
Joe Chmill, Eastman Kodak
Barbara Christiansen
Tony Christopher, Landmark Entertainment
Dominik Clark
David Clayton-Thomas, Blood, Sweat & Tears
Rich Clemmensen, Ethel M Chocolates, Inc.
Bethany Coffey, Huntington Press
David Cohen, CPI
Ron Cole, Reno Air
Valerie Conner
Chanda Cook, Nevada Power Co.
Phil Cooper, Caesars Palace
Alice Cornel
Larry Cox, LVMPD
Maureen Crampton, Forum Shops
Rick Crawford
Michael Crawford, EFX
Frank Cristiano
Chip Croop, Treasure Island
Andrew Crossen, Treasure Island
Fawn Cunningham, Santa Fe Hotel
Gina Cunningham, Bally's
Maura Carey Damacion, Collins San Francisco
Davey-O, A Little Off The Top
Tracey Davis
Scott Dawes, Stratosphere Corp.
Sandra Delapp, Landmark Entertainment
Barb Dennis
Sophie Deprez
Sally Dewhurst, Cirque du Soleil
Greg Diamond, Big Dogs
Mario Diaz, KNTV
Jan Dillard, Las Vegas Stars
Dean Dilullo, Rio Suite Hotel & Casino
Dina DiMercurio
Bill Doak
Don Dobson, The Plaza
Wendy Dombrowski, Mirage Resorts, Inc.
Rob Dondero, R&R Advertising
Julie Drahos, Luxor
Debra Duchane, Sahara
Bob Dunkel
François Dupuis, Mystère
Paul Endy, Paul-Son Gaming Supplies
Paul & Marion Eidsmore
Buck Elsmore, Jr.
Entertainment Tonight
Justina Ercole, Treasure Island
Pam Erickson

Doug Erosky, Sign Systems Inc.
Joanne Eshow, Las Vegas Hilton
Tina Essegian
Betty Eubank, Sporting House
Keith Evans
Louise Faure, San Remo Hotel
Alan Feldman, Mirage Resorts, Inc.
Todd Fisher, Debbie Reynolds Hotel
Joel Fishman, Bally's
Charlie Fitzgerald, Loomis
Bob Fleming, FAA McCarran Airport
June Flowers, Huntington Press
Carol Foster, Bank of America
Robin Foster, Photo Finish
David Friend, LIFE Magazine
Sandy Frye, Eagle Graphics
Al Garcia, American Express
P. Garland Minor
Jesse Garin
George Garrison, Treasure Island
Big Gary, Clubhouse Tavern
Jackie Gaughan
Michael Gaughan
Ellen Georgiou
Carl Gibbs
Chris Gill, Calypso Imaging
Linda Gilleard, LVCVA
Colleen Gleason
Karen Gordon-Borgia, U. M. C.
Joann & Knud Gotterup
Michael Goudeau
Robert & Vera Goulet
Jennifer Grace, Collins San Francisco
Michael Green, B & H Photo
Barbara Greenspun, LV Sun
Sgt. Greg McCurdy, LVMPD
David Grossman
Cathy Guyot, Rio Suite Hotel & Casino
Albert H. Gaynor, Alpha CD Imaging
John Hanks, McCarran Int'l. Airport
Cathy Hanson, City of Las Vegas
April Harrold, Bally's
William Hart, Paul-Son Gaming
Joe Hawk, LV Review-Journal
George Helm
Haley Hertz, What's On?
Diane Hertz, Normandie Motel
Joe Hicks, Sprint
Scott Higgenson
Bob Hirsch, Nevada Film Comm.
Misty Hocker, Photo Finish
Arline Hong, Big Dogs
Larry Houck, Imperial Palace
Roger Hoyt
Jim Hrisoulas
Wayne "Benny" Hronek, Mystère
Bub Hubbard
Jim Huntley, Sands
Ron Hussey
David Hutson
C. J. Powell
Don Jacobs, Entertainment Tonight
Jamie James, James Agency
Bobbi Janus
Laura Jean Wilkins
Jennifer Jenkins, Sporting House
Jackie, Jerry & Arlander Wesley
Linda Jolly, Bank of America
Erik Joseph
Erica Jung
Joe Kaminski
Karen Kane, Sam's Town
Jay Kelbley, Eastman Kodak
Sheriff Jerry Keller, LVMPD
Vicky Kenner
The Kern Family
Nicholas Khoury, Calypso Imaging
Victor Kirschbaum
Ron Kirsh, Explosive Media
Dave Kirvin, Brener Zweikel & Assoc.
Penny Knapp
Doug Kohl

Ken Kragen, Kragen & Company
Bob Kreiger, Lorsch
Myron Kuchman, Golden Nugget
Richard L. Peters
Chuck La Mote
Mr. & Mrs. Stuart Lamb
Jania Lambert, Rio Suite Hotel & Casino
Janice Lane, Liberace Foundation
Connie Lansdown, Sam's Town
Celeste Lantz, A Little Off The Top
Teri Laursenat
Stephanie Lawrence
Don Lawson, Golden Nugget
Michael Leach, DFR
Carol Lee
Lynn Leighton, Sam's Town
Laura Lewis, A Little Off The Top
Lisa Liberati, Bugs & Rudy
Ellen Liebenson, GSI
Terry Lindberg, Flamingo Hilton
Stephen Linder, Household Bank
Tracy Little
Don Logan, Las Vegas Stars
Donna London
Barbara Love, Tropicana
Jim Lovelace

LVCVA Board of Directors:
Commissioner Paul Christensen, Chmn.
Mayor Robert Groesbeck, Vice-Chmn.
Commissioner Lorraine Hunt, Secty./Treas.
Robert Boughner
Mayor Ken Carter
Donald Givens
Councilman Theron Goynes
Marilyn Gubler
Councilman Frank Hawkins Jr.
Mayor Jan Laverty Jones
Barry Shier
David Smith

LVCVA Executive Staff:
Manuel J. Cortez, Pres. & CEO
Rossi Ralenkotter, Vice Pres., Marketing
William Hammond, Vice Pres., Operations
Tom Smith, Vice Pres., Facilities

Kevin Lynch
Ann Lynch, Sunrise Hospital & Medical Cntr.
Carol Maalouf, Treasure Island
Don Maclean, Cirque du Soleil
Douglas Madeley, Calypso Imaging
Chuck Maffia, Bank of America
Troupe Maison, Mystère, Cirque du Soleil
Frank Mallie, Calypso Imaging
Tom Mangione, First Interstate Bank
Annmarie O'Kane, Mirage Resorts, Inc.
Greg & Birgit Marshall
Heather Marshall
Nathan Marshall
Ray Marshall
Karen Marshall, Nevada Dev. Authority
Myron Martin, Liberace Foundation
Shannon Martin, Treasure Island
Pat Marvel, LV Hilton
Andrea Matz
Mike Mauros
The McAlpin Family
Roberta McCann, DRGM
Glenda McCartney, Nevada Power Co.
Mike McCartney, KLVX-TV
Kristi McElyea, Luxor
James McGlasson, Showbiz
Magna Media International
Doug Mehring
Jennifer Meinen
Mike Mesner
Lois Meyerson
Shirley Meyerson
Ross Meyerson
Graham Meyerson
Jennifer Michaels, Mirage Resorts, Inc.

Gary Miereanu
John Mihalka, Eastman Kodak
Robin Miller, Hot Rock N Country
Rick Moffit, Flying Elvi
Toni Molloy-Tudor
Donald Moore, Springtime Prod.
Marie Moretti, Sam's Town
Genevieve Morgan
LaDene Morton
Snow Mtn. Paiute Reservation
Barbara Mulholland, Citibank
Debbie Munch, Caesars Palace
Howard Murray
Joseph Mutti Travel Services
Art Nadler, LV Sun
Karen Nelson Bell, Country Tonight
Keith Nelson, Springtime Prod.
John Neumiller, Sam's Town
Emily Newberg, Lied Museum
Lorraine Noonan, U.M.C.
Phil Norbert, Jr., Rio Suite Hotel & Casino
John Norton, KLAS-TV
Yolanda Nufiez
Norm Nusbaum
Blue O'Brien, Calypso Imaging
Clare O'Brien, McCarran Int'l. Airport
Mike O'Callaghan, LV Sun
Clydine O'Conner
Al O'Neil, Southwest Gas
Brian O'Reilly
Anne O'Sullivan
Michele Olivas, Entertainment Tonight
LaVerne Olson
Cooper Olson
Judy Olson, Borders Books
Andrew Olson, Magna Media
Brad Packer, Mirage Resorts, Inc.
Linda Paniagua
Toby Parker
Todd Parks, KLAS-TV
Tom Pastor, Musicians Union #368
Sean Patrick
Rodney Patten, EMS
Don Payne, Media Link
Donna Penka, Treasure Island
Penn & Teller
Sandy Perez
Kari Perin, Collins San Francisco
Frank Pesce
Justin Peters
Jennifer Petersen
Harry Petrie, FAA / McCarran Airport
Jody Piecy
Ken Plonski
Roxie Ponder
Jay Pott
Jim Powers, Mirage Resorts, Inc.
Haskin Press
Goodwin Production Group
Dave Prybylowski
Patrick Putnam
Sue Putnam, Reno Air
Darrin Race
Yvonne Racz, Mystère
Mary Rafalowski, Sam's Town
Sarah Ralston, Circus Circus Ent., Inc
Jon Ralston, LV Review-Journal
Dany Reidy, Planet Hollywood
Debbie Reynolds
Ted Reynolds
Mark Rich, The Hop
Charlotte Richards
Kelly Ringelberg, Arizona Charlie's
Cindy Rober
Blair Rodman
Kenny Rogers
Sig Rogich
Linda Rongo
Connie Ross, Imperial Palace
Leslie Rossman
Mike Roth, Planet Hollywood
Barbara Rowell

Rondi Rowland, Mirage Resorts, Inc.
Max Rubin
Kathi Rusconi, Sundance Helicopters
Chuck Ruthie, Boyd Gaming
Elliott Sackler, Sprint
Marianne Samenko, Eastman Kodak
Glenn Schaeffer, Circus Circus Ent., Inc
Robert Schear
Patricia Schell
Shirley Scheller
Ken Schick, Calypso Imaging
Nathan Scott, Treasure Island
Jim Seagrave, Stardust
George & Lex Selland
Israel Serrato
Sheri Shelton, Photo Finish
Kathy Shepard, Hilton Gaming
Mark Shepard, Mark Shepard Photography
Lee Sido, UNLV Journalism Dept.
Siegfried & Roy
Attention Sign Company.
Drew Silver, Sprint
Matthew Sjoquist, Sands
John Skarapoulos, La Barca
Bob Smith
Christopher Smith, Boyd Gaming
Mark Smith, LV Chamber of Commerce
Katie Soffy
Rick Sorenson, IGT
Joe Speck, The Flying Elvi
George Starsenic, Riviera
Sydney Stein, HSC
Dennis Stein, Nevada Dev. Authority
Marc Stelzer
Ira David Sternberg, Tropicana
Rob Stillwell, Lady Luck
Anne Stovell
Randy Straff, Debbie Reynolds Hotel
David Stratton, Riviera
Howard Stutz, Bally's
Conrad Sudduth, City of Scotts Valley
Jeane Sugarman
John Sullivan, Sundance Helicopters
John & Pauline Sundermeier
Christophe Suszek, Mystère
Lee Swartz, Photo Finish
Stephanie Syrop
Wayne Tanaka
Jack Taylor, MDS
Michelle Tell
David Tempongko
Pasquale, Teresa & Eda Mauro, Teresa's Mfg.
Sandy Thompson, LV Sun
Steve Thueson
Bill Tolliver
Travel-Holiday
Clyde Turner, Circus Circus Ent., Inc.
John Twardowski, McCarran Int'l Airport
Don Usherson, Legends in Concert
Henry V. Hauser
Carole Vandermeyde, Collins San Francisco
Billy Vassiliadis, R&R Advertising
Johnny Verhagen
Denise Vetter, Landmark Entertainment
Jacques Villeneuve
Barney Vinson, Caesars Palace
Mike Walter, Household Bank
Theresa Welch
Pam Wheeler
Dorothy Whitaker
Chrisse White, Sheraton Desert Inn
Don Williams, Paul-Son Gaming
John Williams, YESCO
Kathy Williams, Howard Hughes Corp.
William Winterstein, Excalibur
Dave Wirsching, Stratosphere Corp.
Wendy Wylegala, Candida Donadio
Steve Wynn, Mirage Resorts, Inc.
Charlie Zobell, LV Review-Journal
Lee Zaichick
Bogdan Zajac, Mystère
Dahlia Zalk, Legends in Concert

ABOVE

twilight view of Interstate 15,
the road to Las Vegas, past three
hotel-casinos at Stateline and two
beyond at Jean, as tourists head to,
and depart from, the gaming
capital of the world.

James Marshall